When

Words

Fail

When Words Fail

poems by
Marianne Klekacz

DANCING MOON PRESS
NEWPORT, OREGON

When Words Fail
copyright © 2009 by Marianne Klekacz
All rights reserved

ISBN-13: 978-1-892076-59-5
Library of Congress Control Number: 2009903381
Klekacz, Marianne
When Words Fail
1. Title; 2. Poetry

Manufactured in the United States of America
Cover design: Karen Downs Design
Cover photo © Roman Krochuk, used by permission
Author photo © Carla Perry

Acknowledgements

Acknowledgements are due to the editors of the following publications where some of these poems first appeared: *A Ray of Hope, CALYX Journal, Cloudbank, Congo Mission, Encore, Fishtrap Anthology 10, M Review, Manzanita Quarterly, Mercury, Perigee, Upon the Heavenly Seas.*

Some of these poems first appeared in the chapbook *Life Science* (National Federation of State Poetry Societies, 2003).

DANCING MOON PRESS
P.O. Box 832, Newport, OR 97365; 541-574-7708
www.dancingmoonpress.com
info@dancingmoonpress.com

FIRST EDITION

For Ben, who makes each thing possible, no matter how improbable it seems.

Language is a cracked kettle on which we beat out tunes for bears to dance to, while all the time we long to move the stars to pity.

--Gustave Flaubert

CONTENTS

III.

IV.

I.

The Heart, Too, Makes Its Own Weather

"Ladies and gentlemen, on your right is Mt. McKinley,
at 20,320 feet, the tallest mountain in North America.
We can't usually see it. It's so tall it makes its own weather."
                                              —*Alaska Airlines captain*

Imagine!—a mountain that gathers
vapor into thunderheads,
generates electrical storms,
swirls blizzards around its crags,
that hides its pinnacle
in self-made clouds and fog.

But on a day like today, that rare day
when the mountain stands alone, shining
in the sunlight, I can see
it points straight to heaven.

Coda for Poetry, That Bandit

"In mask, Poetry steals a horse and laughs."
                    George Venn, "Poetry, That Bandit"

When Poetry rode up on his stolen horse, I laughed
out loud. The sway-backed nag had bony withers,
splayed hooves, spavined hocks, her ribs a hair-covered
xylophone. Her head hung down as she nibbled
the sparse grass, waiting. "Poetry!" I cried,
"Why ever did you steal such a horse?"
Sheepishly he answered, "If you want to steal a horse,
you have to catch it first. She's slow."

He lifted me onto the horse's back behind him,
me anxiously waiting for the poor, sad beast
to collapse under our combined weight.
Then Poetry's horse leaped into the sky.

4

An Angle Explains Euclid

Well, he said, I am acute,
and when I find my complement,
together we'll be right.
We can multiply ourselves.
The square root of the added result
is a long line joining our sides.
We will not be equal, unless
each is a perfect 45. Congruence
is achieved only through bifurcation.

That angle won't find a complement.
He's obtuse. His mother says so.
His oversized ego leaves little room
for a companion.

The interior angle is constrained. His equal
opens opposite, facing another direction.
There is a point at which they meet,
but they can never work together.

My vertex is a point. You can't see
a point, but put enough together
and you get a line. Spin the line,
you get a circle, arriving where it started.
Spin the circle, you get a sphere.
In three dimensions,
that's all you need to know.

Linguistics

Oh, I want to be a vowel,
to form a perfect sound by myself—
A. E.   I
find even when short,
vowels are versatile.
Eh?
Ah-h-h-h. . .

Consonants are hangers-on, completely
uttered only when joined to a vowel.
The liquidity of *m-m-m* and *n-n-n,*
the resonance of *l-l-l-* and *r-r-r,* deceive.
Radiator, register, reservoir—
so much depends on the vowels.

Some consonants demand.
They bring us to a complete stop,
b, p, k;
without vowels we can't even say their names—
bee, pee, kay—you see?

Some consonants aspire.
f-f-f, h-h-h, s-s-s—
nothing more than strong breath sounds,
windy emptiness.

I'd look for another vowel,
one willing to be a diphthong,

my O to his I, perhaps.
Together, we could reconnoiter,
loiter in the park,
anoint our bodies with lotion,
boil up a potion,
embroil ourselves in commotion,
toil over a memoir.
My avoirdupois would please him;
we'd carry equal weight.

There's no risk of elision
when two vowels join.

Pousse Café

"Only a true mixologist can do this,"
the bartender said. *"You have to know
the specific gravity of each liqueur, which
will rise above the other, not become
distracted by the powerful aromas.
A challenge for the drinker, too, to taste
each layer separately, not churn them
into muddy sludge."*

Joy floats, its clear brilliance swimming
across the top of golden hope,
lighter even than pink laughter effervescing
upward from amusement and amazement,
lighter than gray stillness left by shock,
the mauve sadness of the weary woman.
Sorrow sinks, a blue stone, decomposes,
rising slightly, licking the edges between
sadness and rusty isolation, roiling, rolling,
poured neatly onto a base of ochre desolation,
the chocolate darkness of despair.

Quantum Thoughts

--Physicist Erwin Schroedinger explained
quantum theory by postulating that if you put a
cat in a container with a particle that has a
random chance of killing it, until the container
is opened and the cat's state determined, the
cat is both alive and dead.

How that hand must have lingered,
a sword suspended,
descending to sever uncertainty.
Did he, angst-ridden, seek to stay
it in midair, hanging by a hair,
to keep the half-life of the box
rather than risk none?

Is it better to be regarded half alive
or half dead? If anyone asked
Schroedinger's cat, history records
no response. But we smell the fear,
the bitter dread that must have filled
the box. He senses the hand draw near,
prepare to lift the lid, display
his fate, his state, dispel
the mystery, expose him finally
as cat or carcass.

A Boy Considers the Movement of Air

He wants to ride the rails
of the wind, hop it like a freight
and whirr along its trails
in the forest, winding through
the leaves and branches, dropping
into the canyon, never stopping,
taking in the sights, light
as a dandelion seed, borne
on vapors, floating.

He wants to raft the rivers
of the air, circumnavigate
his world, all sails unfurled
and stretched, move with currents
only he can feel.

He wants to rise, cast away
the weight of his body, become
an atmospheric phenomenon.
He wants to be a hurricane
in the Atlantic, a typhoon in the Pacific,
far from places people live, of course,
not to hurt anyone, just to know
the power of his own breath.

North of Harrisburg

I sped along back roads in blackness.

When the sky began to glow, I thought,
Salem must be burning down.
But a gash of mint slashed through,
as if flung by palette knife or brush.

Aurora borealis.

I leapt from the car
into a night of a thousand
green flames flickering
across a deep rose sky.

I raised my arms in the ionized air,
the skin between my fingers
electrified and throbbing.

Then there was no I, no sky.
I let the universe rush into me.

In my own great flowering,
I rose to meet the stars
and lost myself in the light.

Early Morning Shower

August:
   Perseid meteors
flash long across 3 a.m.
    indigo.
A nascent moon hangs
in flaming needle-sharp spray,
turning
       white
           shoulders.

Pinky toes. . .

. . .are unimportant anatomical appendages
until you hurt one. Everyone knows
the importance of the big toe, the honcho,
the one you balance with, the loss
of which can throw you off forever.

Not so the pinkie—just there, sometimes
curled a bit into your foot
from savage shoes, a horny toenail
an out-of-control cuticle—a real pain,

especially when it's broken.

Then you find how present it really is,
each wincing movement evidence
of some once higher purpose, like
the hooked vestigial tail at the end of your spine—
you don't know it's there until
it gets a good whack, then
you think of little else for months—
or the shriveled appendix
that serves no purpose
but can still threaten your life when inflamed,
septic, or ruptured, demanding immediate attention.

All those unimportant things—how they command
our obeisance, our respect. Like cats, perhaps,
giving little, demanding all
the grace we have to give.

Jazz Is a Small Town

Afternoons, Clarinet whispers
across the fence to Saxophone, gossip,
innuendo to noodle away the day.
Saxophone laughs a raucous response,
startling Bass, who idles down
the street, back-lit, hand in hand
with Piano. Shadows lengthen. Drum rattles
his stick along the pickets, shuffles
through the leaves, thrums his basketball, a beat
that drives the sun behind the shed. Light
fades out, lamps come on, Trumpet calls
the night, a lonely wail, one long, blue hush.

And in the dark the slithery things
come out, the ones that crawl along
your spine, the tingle and the tickle,
the itch that doesn't quite,
the quick movement just beyond
your field of vision, flash
of almost insight right outside,
and you shiver,
and hear the slide of sidewalks
rolling up the scale as,
secreted by the sound,
Mr. Baxter beats his wife,
the burglar breaks a window
in the Hammond's empty house,
the tinkle of glass on grass

buried in the heartbeat of the street
laid bare now and shining as the moon
rises over smoking chimneys
and the breath of autumn's chill.

And somewhere, somebody's
baby is crying—"wah, wah, wah"—
blue, blue, blue. At 3 a.m.
the slow wail startles, cracks
the hush of night, shatters
reverie and sleeplessness.
A hopeless song, a song
of all the wrongs in the world.

Hungry, lonely—those are the lyrics,
and this is the music to set them to.
But wait—another note, one swift
lullaby intrudes and soothes.
The street begins to breathe
again and in the east
a slow, dull light awakens.

Mozart and Memory

"And I am alive in the midst of so much forgetting."
                    Pablo Neruda, "Return to a City"

Mozart wrote too many notes.
You think you're listening to a melody
when a sudden arpeggio, an unexpected
flute wanders off into another plane.

How many times I wished you not
dead, perhaps, but disappeared, and here,
ten years after you were buried
in the earth, an errant flute recalls

an afternoon of sunlight on a lake,
a Nietzschean day of nothing
definite, and everything,
what seemed like forever at the time.

That's the trouble with Mozart.
You're going smoothly with the music
and the tone shifts, a divergent song appears,
your mind goes somewhere else.

II.

Mme. Lazarus

When Granny crawls out of the hooch, her body
sieve-like, riddled with one-inch shrapnel,
I know. I know by your quickened breath,
by the grinding of your teeth. I wrap my arms
around you tightly, draw you back from that sullen,
sultry southeast Asia jungle where you are once again
realizing all of your medical skills can't save her, even
as she whispers softly in Vietnamese,
"I am all right. I am all right."

Your dreams have given her a sort of immortality.
Nightly, you resurrect her, helpless, hopeless
against her ghost, your grenade launcher
spent and accusing at your feet.

What the Medic Was Thinking

Cu Chi Province, Vietnam, 1968

Blood—oh, God, there is so much blood!
Why is the chopper taking so long?
I'd carry him out on my back if I could.

How could a mission go so wrong?
A man can't lose this much blood and live.
Why is the chopper taking so long?

I've given him all I have to give.
Others are waiting, calling for help.
A man can't lose this much blood and live.

Shrapnel wounds from knee to scalp—
I really should give him up for dead.
Others are waiting, calling for help.

But still he breathes. "I'm cold," he says.
I cover him, search his eyes, and wait.
I really should give him up for dead.

I know the chopper will come too late.
I cover him, search his eyes, and wait.
I'd carry him out on my back if I could.
Blood—oh, God, there is so much blood!

Slipping Into War

Like forgotten objects on a dark staircase,
words trip us up,
transforming themselves between
your mouth and my ears. A long fall,
accelerating to a disastrous end.
Talk is *not* cheap; language used
indiscriminately is a slippery seducer.

How easily our ideological
disagreement draws its guns, points
in threat, rational aim
forgotten. Argument fires
our brains, dulls our restraint.
What began as discussion, dissension,
ends in destruction, real blood flowing,
pooling at our surprised feet.

Lost Innocence

I should've bought it
before I left
to learn
to kill.
I knew I should.

When I came home,
my son cried,
"Daddy!"
then drew back
afraid of the uniform.

He hid in his mother's skirts.
I left and drove
straight to the house
I should've bought,
ancient apple tree in the yard,
so right for climbing,
for a swing.

Still there,
still vacant,
the apple tree
fruited out, the ground
covered with apples,
a bite from each one,
and buzzing with wasps.

I looked up,
and on a branch
saw black evil eyes,
the razor teeth of a scavenger,
waiting, watching.

My gorge rose
at all that spoiled fruit.
I drew my .45, climbed
and brought the enemy down.

At the Wall

I.

The rain falls steadily now, strikes the granite,
sluices down in waves, obscuring the names carved there.
He stands before the Wall, in fatigues faded
from many washings, wet once more, as he was wet
in the jungle 31 years ago. "1969"
is graven deeply in the stone before him,
deeper still in his memory. He steps forward
suddenly, swipes the water from a single name,
now sharp in relief against the black slab.

His cheeks are wet. I want to taste his face,
to know—is this the bitter salt of loss,
or simply cleansing rain he wears?

II.

Midday: the rain stops abruptly.
Steam rises from this rock like ectoplasm ascending.
They are recorded here, these 58,000 souls,
enough to populate the city of Corvallis, or
with their wives and husbands and 2.2 children
never to be born, the cities of Eugene, Salem.
The sun dries the stone, the names reemerge
chisel-sharp in clarity, matching the memories
etched on those who remain.

III.

A walk along the path that hugs the Wall
is a walk through grief, bare and unashamed.
The brightness of the burnished orange trees,
the late October sun cannot light the gray inside,
cannot chase away the night descended so abruptly.
As I watch, shades seem to step from the polished surface.
I know these are reflections, yet still I view this sad parade;
I want to salute, but I don't. Across the centuries, I feel
Jason's shock—only the mad devour their young.

One Lone Quince Blossom

November 22, 2003

Take it out, I said to the yard man,
cut it back to nothing. It's a weed.
And he did. Just stubs remain.

I'm upstairs putting in
the third load of laundry.

Forty years ago, I sat
in a gas station in Weed, California,
in the back seat of Emma Lee's
pale green 1962 Cadillac, its obscene
fins adding nearly a foot to its length,
with Virginia, who would become
my mother-in-law. "The President,"
the radio announcer said, "has been shot
in Dallas. His condition is unknown."

The forecast for today was "partly sunny,"
but snowflakes have been falling
since morning. From the laundry room
I see the backyard, and there
a single coral quince blossom
blooms against the unpainted garage.

In April, this would be unremarkable,
but suddenly, I am crying.

Late Night at the Battered Women's Shelter

Three pale faces peer
from behind the folds of a loose
cotton skirt, humped high
in the middle, evidence that soon
a fourth will follow. The eyes, all six,
are wide enough to fall into,
black against ashen skin,
the flesh of fear reflected
to my gaze. Her eyes are shallow,
empty, zombie eyes.

Tomorrow, fed, safe for the moment,
perhaps she will smile, breathe
more deeply in unconstrained air.

Tonight, she smothers in the weight
of not her belly but her responsibility—
five lives bundled in a cotton dress,
a simple dress with pink flowers
and a crooked brown stain
where her lip bled down.

All she owns
she carries on her back.

Marginalia

She constructed the text of her life
with care, laid out the plot
in punctuated chapters, good
schools, a suitable marriage,
two steps up the social ladder,
and 2.5 children,
years later, long after,
regretting the .5—
the blood dried, the cramps
and swelling just faint memory
like a song once heard
on a sunny afternoon
and recalled as rain drizzles down.

Nothing wrong with the .5 child except
bad timing. Shaky marriage, career
taking off, no time to be pregnant.
So he (she's sure it was the son
she never had, her daughters are attentive
but she always wanted a boy
someone to play with trucks
and guns and scare the neighbors
with his chopped and flaming hot
rod) had to go. She edited him out,
a little let-down afterward, hormones
the doctor said, be patient.

It was the right decision, she knows
it was, so why now
as she gives her text a final edit
does she see ".5" ".5" written
everywhere? She has spoiled—
by scribbling in the margins—
a perfectly good first edition

11 O'clock News

A tale of three women

I.

She lies amid humus and leaf rot
in Forest Park.
Her half-clothed body sprawls,
ragdoll-like, decaying,
less than it once was,
more than it will be again.
Her eyes stare vacantly
into the green canopy overhead.
Her spirit is gone.
What she was to be is in her past,
her flesh washed
again and again,
prepared for burial
by the relentless rain.
The youngest deputy averts his gaze.
Older, more experienced men,
leaden-eyed,
go about the business of marking
measuring, photographing.

II.

She sits in the dressing room at the TV station.
From the mirror, her nearly naked body
watches as she picks up the tear sheets.
The identity of the body found today
in Forest Park has not been released. Police speculate…

She tosses the tear sheets on the vanity,
smiles her practiced smile, then frowns
at flaws revealed, the sag here, the laugh wrinkles
crinkling her careful makeup. Thank God for the lights
at the Brasserie. She will look 25 again
for her after-show meeting with the producer.
Which neckline will support her microphone best?
The bright lights accentuate
the bones beneath her skin.

III.

She sits soporific on the sofa,
soothed by the suckling
of her daughter at her breast.
The news broadcast flickers flashes
and shadows around the darkened room.
The volume is low; she cannot hear
the words of the carefully groomed
young woman on the screen. She shifts
the baby, wondering about the future.
A change in the light recalls her attention.
On-the-spot television crews are filming
the site of the latest Forest Park murder.
She watches the police remove the body.
Someone's sister? Someone's mother?
Someone's daughter? She grasps
her daughter so tightly that
the baby stops nursing until, reassured,
she breathes the barest sigh, begins to suckle again,
leaving her mother to face the fear alone.

Back to Normal

Manhattan, September 20, 2001

The homeless man recites a list, today's
disasters, restaurants closed, dumpsters devoid
of discarded food, effluence of the affluent.
He scuttles along the sidewalk, muttering to
himself, casts sideways looks at empty streets—
no eye contact, no change to spare, just rain.
He sees but does not register the bright
vests of the workers moving slowly across
the mounds of concrete, steel, sidles past
the charnel house, crosses himself, crosses
the street. A Pinkerton man waves him on.
He skitters off in search of shelter, supper,
unseeing, unseen, a scavenger of the city,
a cockroach from the cupboard caught in the light.

Chicken

You languish there in Plato's cave,
    watching shadows as substance,
        hearing echoes as oracles.

You are fettered by chains you refuse
    to release, frightened of freedom,
        swallowed by the dark.

The fires of life burn behind you,
    but you will not look, you will not
        turn to face the light.

If you would leave the cave's darkness,
    you must climb the broken shale,
        the uncertain upward slope.

If all you know of chickens is a shadow,
    what can you know
        of feathers, of eggs?

A Pocketful of Change

"... *a good time to carry a poem in your pocket.*"

Billy Collins, NPR Morning Edition,
April 1, 2003

Is there a *bad* time, a time we don't need
the sheaf of 3x5 cards tucked away,
the notebook a rustle of dried leaves
that would whirl away in wind without
the spiral binding that holds them fast?

A time that we don't need lilacs, or orioles,
miracles and mysteries, the first force
of spring emerging from Earth's frozen crust?
A time we don't need madrigals or arias,
crickets chirping in the fainting light?

If so, I haven't found it yet.
When you are needy come to me,
and I will turn my pockets inside out,
let the breeze carry my words,
my scattering of change, to your ears.

III.

When Words Fail

I can only tell you
about Christmas morning, 1957,
how I awoke at 3 a.m., too excited
to sleep, to the queer silence that follows
a heavy snow, the streetlights reflecting
on its shining surface, lighting
my windows like early dawn,
how I crept downstairs with the flashlight
I hid the night before,
opened the sliding door, slowly, hoping
it would not creak as it often did,
slipped through the opening
and tiptoed to the tree, my torch stroking
the silver blades, red slats of a Flexible Flyer,
just like the one in the window
at Gurdy's True Value Hardware Store,
the sled that for weeks had drawn me
six blocks out of my way each day
to pass that window with a sideways
glance, dragging my toes, never brave enough
to go inside and touch the unattainable,
how I stood and stared, some great atomic
reaction welling up within, how, fearful
I might explode, I retraced
my footsteps, returned to bed,
to hug myself and grin
until daylight, already flying.

Blackberry Fiend

A blackberry in the mouth is worth
two on the bush. It slides so sweetly
onto the tongue, oblivious to fate,
then, yielding up its juices, fills my mouth
with its warm nectar.

                                    I ate
a pint or more last time I picked,
luxuriant in the silky moisture trickling
down my throat, sunshine running through
me, turning my mouth purple until
I looked like a vampire sated by a lover's blood.

Juicy, replete, I sprawled in the tall grass,
staining the neat white daisies
with dripping evidence of my greed.

First Love

I rode its drop the way
the river rides its summer bed—
tumbling over rough and rocky spots,
with flashes of brilliance
and a soft murmuring, pooling
in the still, deep places,
then rushing on
answering some tidal call.

Like the river, it ended in a salt marsh,
fed by tears.

Acoustics

Ernst Chladni discovered it second,
how bowing produced resonance,
harmonics, left lines and patterns
on a previously pristine surface,
how tonal irregularities marked
his smooth sand. Hooke found it first,
nearly two centuries earlier,
with glass and flour instead
of metal and sand, discovered the center,
272 beats per second, middle C,
in "the Scale of all Musick."

I have rediscovered this,
how internal vibration changes
the shape of my lips, my eyes
widening to near circles;
how a note well struck can mold
my body, straighten or arch my back,
tighten my breasts, leave my arms
reaching, reaching. . .

Chladni left thousands of drawings
documenting concentric circles,
spokes of wheels within wheels, webs,
always in even-numbered divisions,
for every wave produces a resonant disturbance
on the other side. In figures of two dimensions,
oddness is precluded.

Today, new crinkles at the edges of my face,
symmetrically arranged, remember
how I quivered when you sang.

Sometimes I Dream of Fireflies

And always we are together, and the night is dark,
a special dark, not black exactly, or navy blue,
or even purple, just dark, and we are engrossed
in each other, not needing sight, when the fireflies
flicker to life like flying, glowing white clover,
blooming, not blooming, blooming, not blooming,
until it feels like the whole world blooms in turns
and the blossoms turn, the sky turns,
the world turns into some other world,
some other universe where we float off amid
those flickering stars that we never would have seen
except for the dark space in the middle of Nebraska in
August, 1982.

Ali Baba's Cave Speaks

Come, my adventuring friend,
and when you reach my door,
only let your eyes say "Open, Sesame,"
and I will bid you enter,
offer up hidden rubies and pearls,
bathe you in radiance of reflected gold.
When you are hungry,
honey nougat and sweet apples;
thirsty, herbed wine from a spring
that freshens to your touch;
tired, enfolding drapes to wrap you
as you rest. I am waiting.

Trophy Wife

Bzzz, BZzz, BZZz . . .
Here is the yellow jacket snared
in a nearly invisible web of silk
an energetic spider has spun across the flowerpot.

The spider clothes the yellow jacket
in new raiment of finest silk.
This will be her shroud.

The spider works deliberately, patiently.
When she is perfectly adorned,
he will sting her with his rich venom,
suck the juices from her body,
withdraw, temporarily sated, waiting.

Chinese New Year

We romped through San Francisco,
driving the dragon, you at the head,
me tailing behind, weaving like two drunks
among the eucalyptus, cypress, Monterey pine,
between the parking meters and under the off-ramps.
Leaving Chinatown to the tourists, we sped
through the Stockton tunnel. You had the eyes,
I followed blindly, trusting
you knew where we were going.
When I tripped on the cable car rail,
we stopped, I emerged and saw
we were in no place I knew,
no place I expected to be.

The whores on Third Street ogled and leered,
winked an invitation, tilted a spike-heeled foot
to spread a naked leg, a come-on,
"Come on, big boy, over here, to Mama.
Come on over here and die a little death."
And the shiny metallic scales fell in a heap
around me as you danced off, the gunshot
bang and tracer lights of firecrackers
dancing with you. When the explosions stopped,
the night was very dark, very still.

In Case You Ever Wonder

This is the final insult. Like a slap,
it lies between us, an angry flat
handprint incalescent in the air.
You never touched me, you wouldn't dare.
Your venom marked me the worse for that.

Those hateful words built a wall, then spat
graffiti upon it, a barrier to separate,
offend, and distance us. I swear,
this is the final insult.

Tomorrow, in the wakening sun, I'll pack
my things and load them in the waiting cab.
And if some evening you should, in black despair,
call out, and want me to be waiting there
to chase the demons, to go on the attack,
remember, *this* was the final insult.

Paralyzed By Regret

I couldn't help the fateful backward glance—
to see my finely draped salon, the figs
in hammered bronze that graced my table.
Perhaps it was the echo of a laugh
that rolled across the plaza late last night.

All of Abraham's sacrifices
will not suffice. Lot pitched his tent
toward Sodom, and on sand,
good intentions shifting, one compromise
leading to another. I goaded him on.

Now the angel's hand bids hurry,
hurry, don't look back, move
steadily on or you will die.
Ahead the safety of the highland;
behind the pleasures of the low.

Divided heart, uncertain will:
I turned to look the way I'd come,
stone falling on stone, oblivion. . .
Now only desiccated tears remain,
salt blown across the landscape of my memory.

Four Phases of the Moon

I.

Too late the moon
slipped behind the rippled ridge
as if below waves, drowning.

Too late. It left
me restless, agitated,
its ghostly afterimage

a memory of the spider web
illuminated such a short time since
now dark, invisible, trembling.

The gravid gibbous form is gone,
taking the white from the apple blossoms
and the tips of alder leaves unfolding.

II.

The moon I'd rather not remember
rose round and pale orange
in the smoke from harvest fires
one evening in October.

It climbed the night
sky unremarked,
incalescent, matching
passion with passion, until

its blue-white fire flooded
through the window, illuminating
the bare shoulder of the man who slept
beside me, illuminating everything.

III.

A crescent hangs above my head
and I am left wondering,

like Alice,
where the body has gone,

what surprise awaits me next
in this unexpected rabbit hole.

IV.

Just a hole in the sky where the moon once was—

Fir trees loom, black on black.

I know them by what is missing.

What Copernicus Knew

If only she'd studied astronomy,
she might have known about double stars,
those bodies of nearly equal mass
and energy, locked in perpetual
double orbit, circling around

each other, always distanced,
always together. If only she'd known
about parallax, how different views
of the same object, magnified
by angles, skewed the separateness.

She might have learned about gravity,
the attractive force kept in check
by balance, how important the distance,
the measurable weight, in the scheme of things.
She certainly might have known.

If she'd only just known what Copernicus knew,
she might have discovered his rising and setting
came from her spinning atilt on her axis,
not from his circling around her, attracted.
The orbit was hers alone.

She might have been warned about lightness of being,
how losing her solidness drew her closer
and closer to fiery destruction. She spun,
casting to space the rocks of her grounding,
her mutable core. If only she had known.

After

The carnations in the vase are fading, slowly starting to look like ghosts. Bright red becomes dusty rose, the pink the palest shadow of itself. Even the white looks, well, less white, less like puffs than faded striations, nearly translucent, weighty cumulous blown into nimbus feathers.

The wind is rattling the fireplace doors, knocking to get in, whistling your code down the chimney. But the glass doors are firmly closed, and I am here in my fuzzy robe, with fuzzy thoughts, alone with the flowers and the vase, remembering when all the colors were clear and fresh, watching dullness descend. A smell like the silence after snow hangs in the air.

The Naming of Cats

It's almost as difficult
as the naming of feelings
or muted colors
that aren't quite true.

Is it mauve or rose,
lilac or lavender,
violet or indigo?

Is it sadness or fear
of death—tristesse—
or simply pensée?

It's best to have
a different language
to blur the edges
to ease the slide
from one to the next,
to bleed the differences
across the page.

You have to start with tone
and go from there.
It would never do
to call Mr. Pugs "Flossie"
or George "Pierre"
or even Kitty "Empress."

It would never do
to mock the loss
of a parent, a child,
to chide grief,
to murmur "It will be
all right" when nothing
ever will be again.

Language is what we have.
It is not enough.

I Think I Want to Tell You Something

I can't remember lots of things.
I can't remember the last time
I remembered what's forgotten.
I can't even remember what
I forgot and I think
I forgot to tell you that.

If only memory were like
my big dictionary, everything
indexed and accessible,
written down in black
on white paper,
black and white,
just that simple.

But it's not,
and if it used to be,
I've forgotten.
I don't remember that sureness,
my certainty of knowing.
Now I just don't know.

I don't remember,
and if I ever did,
I've forgotten.

Aquifer

We absorb stubbed toes,
broken bones and hearts,
disappointments, harsh words
heard and said,
filter them through gravelly time,
fine sand of experience,
store them on bedrock,
still, clear reservoir
unseen until, when needed most,
expected least, it bubbles up
through surface cracks,
artesian strength.

IV.

Less Than Nothing is Still Something

Even a negative is positive.
Minus one is what we have left
if we've given away more than we have,

borrowed more than we should,
said one too many goodbyes,
set a place at the table for Aunt May

forgetting that she died in 2002.
Uncle George is not surprised.
He says he forgets all the time.

Minus one is the minute before
the one in which we should have acted,
or something less than enough.

If x = -1, you question the sufficiency
of what you hold, its weight, its heft,
the specific gravity of the thing.

You might question its place in the world,
its meaning in what is left.
But you know its existence is real.

You Notice It First in the Eyes

They widen, then freeze, as he struggles
to follow the ribbon of memory through eyelet
in his brain, discovers the ribbon cut,
the tenseness as he searches for the word
that says just what he means, the word
that was there last week, there yesterday.
His jaw stiffens and grinds, as if his mouth
could call forward what thought cannot.
Only his pain, his fear are fully connected—
"I keep forgetting things," he says.

And he does. This is not losing his car keys,
his glasses. This is losing access to 65 years,
experience that has guided him
as surely as a rudder steers a ship,
a steering wheel a car. Without this,
he is adrift in a fog bank, careering
helplessly down a curving road.
This is dangling over a dark
and frightening precipice, holding on tightly,
feeling his grip slip.

Hang on with him. Three years or twenty?
The doctors don't know,
He will be excited, then tearful,
nostalgic for—what?—then remote.
The numbers in his checkbook mutate
into hieroglyphics. His shoes don't match.
His feet hurt; he has on two left shoes.
He has forgotten how to tie them.

One day he will not recognize you.
The first time is the worst,
denying 40 years of friendship,
of intimacy. Hug him frequently,
lest he forget the warmth of human touch.

The day will come
when he is at peace, if you are not,
when the fear becomes resignation.
He will slide quietly through each day,
always in the present, no longer bothered
by tasks unfinished, books unread.
Each sunrise will be fresh and new,
the only one he remembers seeing.

You will mourn alone.
He will know no loss.

Replay

Her fear comes from forgetting.
The whirring wears away the memories.
She had believed them fixed, those thoughts,
a movie that looped through her brain.

But the edges of the film are worn now,
and sometimes her inner projector seizes,
the screen flickering on a single image,
sometimes golden, sometimes black.

Then she rewinds the last few
frames and starts the old machine
again, holding her breath
as the stiff film catches in the cogs.

She knows the time will come
when the old machine won't start,
when the loop will hang
on a single recovered image.

Each time she splices, she loses
a few frames here, a few frames there,
a blurred transition, a jerk.
Whatever remains will define her life.

Beauty

The woman in front of me
at the pharmacy is filling her prescription
for PremPro. "I don't care what they say
about the dangers of hormone replacement,"
she says to her friend, "This makes me look
younger." I can't determine her age.
Her skin is smooth, where unwanted hair
has been lasered away, her face impassive still
from last week's Botox injections.

I think about how other generations
used belladonna to brighten the eyes,
arsenic to whiten the skin, how my own
thought the best sign of vital good health
was a dark glowing tan. We mixed iodine
into the baby oil to hasten the process.
Years later, we had the deadly cankers
cut away, if we discovered them in time.

I think about my grandmother at 80
how her eyes crinkled just before she laughed,
the sudden spark a warning of prank to come.
I see her smiling when the bread was kneaded
and rising, the garden tended, the table
crowded with chattering children come to visit.
I think of her preserving the food she grew,
testing each glass jar carefully,
knowing botulism can sicken, can kill.

Returning After Decades of Separation

Worn linoleum shows the kitchen
its backing, asbestos and fiber.
Peeling wallpaper hangs,
long strips crawling
down the dining room walls.

Stunned by the decay, I walk
through the kitchen and dining room,
watched warily by my former husband
and his current wife.
I approach the glassed-in porch
where his mother sits.

She nods pleasantly, smiles vacantly,
doesn't recognize the woman
she called daughter for 15 years.

Inside her brain, the doctors say,
are lesions and holes. I picture them
like the worn-through linoleum,
the drooping and torn wallpaper.

In time the house will fall down.
For the moment there's just this
slow-motion disintegration.

Winter Solstice

Night comes early, and stays
long. Tired
of this season of death—
the dead grandchild, the dying friend,
the brother gravely ill—

I want to imitate the tulip
and crawl deep into my bed,
pull the comforter over me
like a rich layer of duff
and wait,
until the sun again warms my earth.

But roots go deep.
I hear my mother's voice—
"You can't fix this, you can
only wait it out."

So I will draw away awhile,
and rest,
and let my roots nourish me
through these dark and dreadful days.

I'll start an amaryllis
in the kitchen window,
to prove that things still grow.

Night Vision
for Tom

I never knew
how beautiful
your hands are.

I have seen them
many times, strong
on the wrench, controlled
in the fly cast, gentle
on Lisa's shoulder or nape,
the small of her back.

But tonight,
as you lie dying,
I discover
this amazing grace—
your hands rise on thin arms
like swans' necks, backlit
by orange mica lamplight,

rising and weaving,
rising and reaching
as you pluck
from the air
above your bed
things only you can see—

birds bobbing on a lake
before a sun-setting sky.

Tar Baby

Like tar, it is, the way bad news
glues my feet, holds me
immobile, all my best guesses
sliding away and I can't follow.

I lift a foot. The black goo
pulls it back and slaps it
down again, still stuck,
slightly different, mostly the same.

I try to free it. My hands
now covered in the mess
that holds me here, I reach
for support. Here I am,

glued to the door jamb,
a hand on each side,
feet on the sill.
No one can get through,

and I can't move,
can't be moved,
can't.

Starry Starry Night

I wanted something
more, I guess—comets
or meteors, some sign,
some evidence
the wind from the sun still blows.

I wanted Van Gogh's vision
of skewed skies and whirling
air above quiet, sleepless
streets, above burning
windows lit for night.

The sky was pomegranate
when you died. Radiant
with unholy light,
it flamed the western hills
in prairie fire, and lit your face.

Now, just this lonely juniper
stands bleak against the blue-
black sky, so still among
these pricks of light that cut
the night, these puny stars.

I wanted something different
from this bitter rusty attar
in my mouth, a gale perhaps,
or summer lightning, something
to mark your passing,
to outline the hole left
in the landscape, this desert,
this dry, abandoned place.
Where are you? If you are
out there in the stars, send me a sign.

Like Swallows Gathering at Summer's End

For Fred Harrison

The equinox approaches. The nestlings,
fledged and flying, rise
above the shadows of the valley floor
to feed on gnats golden
in late afternoon sun.

A long journey lies ahead.
They will fly together, survive
separately, to reach or not
some warm place
in California or Mexico,
sybarites abandoning winter.

The smallest would rather play
than eat. He spirals higher than the rest,
then dives among the others
in freefall, scattering them,
climbs again and dives, and again.
I feel his secret amusement
from the meadow where I stand watching.
I hope he survives the trip.

Tomorrow or the next day
other nests will come, one, then another,
then another until
the sky is filled
with the swirling of birds.

Then they will be gone,
this gathering of migrants,
lifting over hills and rivers,
resting briefly in a strange forest,
not to be seen again until spring.

At the memorial service, a vision—
I see him like that, rising
above the shadows that dogged
his last weeks, joining friends
who have made this trip before,
offering a wink, a laugh,
greeting them with silly names,
a quick inviting dance step,
a tug at his ascot,
off to play away the winter,
all days golden now.

Abscission

I.

Surrounded by boxes and trunks, she longs
for the alder's genetic certainty.
In February, sap rushes upward,
drawn from roots deep in the earth,
surges through farthest limbs to swelling buds.

Daily, no, hourly, the alder changes
as green unfurls, opens to the sun.
New branches sprout, new leaves;
without these the alder would explode
from its own life force.

All summer, the tangled canopy
offers shade, concealed habitat,
light music in the wind.
As the sun lowers its arc,
there comes a time of decision—
which leaves are vital to survival?

To the rest, the alder cuts off nourishment;
green disappears, leaving yellows and browns
that were hidden by photosynthesis.
Nonessentials drop away, cast off.
Those spared feed the inner core, build strength
for dormancy in the long winter to come.

II.

The contents of an 8-room house
will not fit in a 4-room apartment.

She must abscise the surplus,
old photos, souvenirs,
a footstool her grandmother rested upon,
the "must have" vase—she never found
the proper flower—Pendleton wool
bought in a fit of ambition not realized.

Books—no, the books must stay,
something else will have to go, perhaps
the good-luck Buddha,
hands upraised in celebration.

How can she choose? The detritus of a life
lived widely lies before her.
Which will offer her shelter, concealment,
warmth in a long winter? Which will fan a spark,
evoke richness, which will sing to her
in the dark days ahead? Which must stay?

The Black Dog

Midsummer days I walk the beach.
The black dog lopes behind.
He's not mine. I won't claim him.
But he follows right along.

He keeps his distance, won't
look at me. Once
I surprised him, turned toward him,
his yellow eyes met mine.
He turned away.

Nights sometimes, I dream
of stepping through the door
into an abyss, or walking
across the meadow into
a sudden chasm, and then
I am falling, falling, and

the falling becomes flying
and I am flying through the black
toward a pair of yellow eyes.
One of them winks. I jolt
awake, thinking:

Not my turn, not yet.

Perspective

Halfway to the top
I find a ledge
and stop. Rappelling
ropes and grapple
hang loosely
from my belt.

Resting, I realize
perspective has changed
my view, my angle,
my line of sight.
The sky blazes blue
and clear. Startling
light shimmers.

The ground below
is just a memory,
wavering in rising heat.

I am only
halfway up.

I had no idea
I was so far down.

V.

Old Friends Like Old Wine

Amico e vino vogliani essere vecchi.
Italian proverb

Some are best consumed
young, and drunk with insouciance,
sangiovese from Carmignano
or primitivo, Beaujolais nouveau, fresh
and alive with the fruit of berries.
These are eminently sippable,
but do not improve with age.
We remember them with sparkle
and a light laugh on the tongue.

But syrah, cabernet, chianti,
Marechal Foch—these linger
in our cellars and on our palates,
open ebulliently to air,
sending out notes of violets and cassis fruit,
sometimes essence of mocha, or cherries.
We consume them on long evenings
of casual talk and unspoken affection,
savoring them to a long, smooth finish.

Class of '62

Banners rustle in the draft of passersby.
Christmas lights wink
at old school chums in search of a party,
or if not a party, a drink will do,
something to subdue the edge of insecurity.

At the 10th, we compared careers,
braggadocio concealing envy, hoped
at least to make the second team,
to play rather than be benched.
At the 20th, we passed around pictures
of sons in football gear, daughters
whose smiles flashed the silver
of orthodontia, beauties to be.
At 30 years, a certain dissatisfaction
crept in. Is this all there is?
Now here we are, 40 years later,
half a lifetime away
from those first steps into maturity.

Candlelight softens the markers of time,
and the eyes have it, that old glow.
The ghosts of old girls and old games hang
in the air, luminous, ectoplasmic
memories floating in the moment.
The DJ starts slowly, then Chubby Checker
strips the worn masks from the faces of teens.

Caught in old music, old moves,
eighteen again, unwilling to abstain,
we twist and shout, jump and spin,
flirt surreptitiously with old loves.
Spouses look on, bored, knowing tomorrow
worn out knees and tender sciatic nerves will complain.
Tonight they don't get a vote. The noise rises, drowning
everything—"Remember?" "Remember?"

The party winds down. We move slowly
toward the door. I turn to look, wondering—
what am I leaving behind?
Then I get it: success is just being here at all.

The music stops, the lights go on,
and age settles like dust across our faces.

Is This What the Artist Intended?

Bound by a gilded frame, the workman walks
an unpaved road, swings a lunchbox
from one hand. His steps are heavy.
Rose light filters through trees that tower
along the road's edges, a suffusion of warm
light across monochromatic shapes.
The man's shoulders are hunched.

We cannot see his face
or even know which way he walks.
His hat brim gives no clue.

In an evening after a long day, I'm sure
he goes home, shoulders slumped in weariness,
light from a dying sun fading in the west.
But mornings his shoulders droop
with dread, the lunch pail weighty in his hand,
his steps reluctant toward some ordeal.
His stride is fixed, forward, resigned.
The light, before or behind, grows steadily.

For twenty years we have argued
about whether this shadow is a collar or a jawline,
the significance of the tilted foot.

Mitosis

Unnoticed, I watch
my daughters at the sink,
Linda up to her elbows in suds,
Mandy waving the dishtowel,
the seventh veil
over her innocence.

How alike, how not alike.
Their blond heads bob
together, giggling.

So soon, the walls of the house
will pinch, and they will separate,
from each other, from me.

Already they are spinning
off on different paths.
Mandy's soccer gear lies
where she dropped it in the hall.
Linda's paints litter the table.

Saturday Night

This week, 48 hours at the Blue Moon Motel,
orange neon sign that trumpets "VACA Y"
("cow and" what, she used to wonder, then found
the burned out "N" and "C"), mop bucket and
dirty sheets from 10 to 6, Monday through Saturday,
energy languishing as she erases the traces
of straw men and women who slept or played here,
preparing the room for the next brazen tryst, the next
furtive tango, gaze averted from the hungover leers
she passes on the walkway, tongue silent
to the jive comments of not-so-secret lechers,
sweeping condoms from corners and filth from everywhere.

But it's Saturday night—40 hours to her next shift.
She slides into the orange salsa dress, ties the ribbons
on her patent leather shoes, ready to jive
when Carlos rounds the corner in his red low-rider Camaro.
She sinks into the bucket seat, pretends to languish
in boredom as he eyes her up and down, everywhere,
secretly pleased as his pupils dilate, his nostrils flare.
The dance club vibrates hot Latin rhythms—mambo,
rumba, lambada, cha cha—his brazen tongue flickers
"Kiss me, here, and here," hers slides up the straw
in her pink dacquiri, answering "Catch me if you can,
corner me and I am yours."

A quick ride
from the dance club to a room where gliding,
whirling, dipping, touching to a slow tango beat,
they tumble, falling through the night
in air of satin and honeysuckle, nectar kisses
piquant with salt from glowing skin,
curves highlighted by faintly blue moonlight
filtering through the dirty *barrio* window.
Monday seems a month away.

Make a Joyful Noise

"Silence before being born, silence after death: life is nothing but noise between two unfathomable silences."
                                    Isabel Allende, <u>Paula</u>

An accident, to be sure, the wrong
medications, too much of one
or another, taken in crisis and pain.
But had it been deliberate,
no surer cut of body, spirit
severed as if by knife,
life rent in two
by blunder or desperation.

To those who talk of angels' song,
I say, "No, no, it's not like that,"
no heavenly host, no holy choir,
no burst of sound to welcome you.
Just light, radiant, white, glowing,
knowing light, all encompassing,
and silence. . .

If it's music you want, make it now.
Erupt in song, a raucous tune.
Learn from the Irish how soon the walk
leads to the grave. Dance your way there,
it takes longer than a steady tread.

Allow improvisation along the way,
a silly pirouette here, a jete' there,
a twist, a dip into a lover's arms,
glissando tango or sprightly two-step—
whatever rhythm you hear.

When the stars sing, hum along.
Better yet, answer them back,
offer a new song, another melody.
There is time enough for silence.

Why I Won't Take Billy Collins's Advice

"There's too much revision going around . . .if
a poem's not working, toss it out and go find
one that is. "

Billy Collins, January 14, 2004

Come on, Billy,
these words deserve respect.
I know they're not working right now,
so I file them in the morgue,
my top file drawer,
with all the other darlings I've killed.

It's not a morgue exactly,
more like a long-term care facility.
They're not on life support—
I've fed them nothing for weeks,
nor breathed any oxygen into them.

They're not dead—comatose, maybe.

I hear them rustling around at night
when I'm trying to sleep.
Who knows, maybe one of these nights
that stunning metaphor I've been saving
will snuggle up against that handsome piece
of meter farther back in the file,
and they'll create something wonderful
while I dream.

The Instrument

Drifting on thermals, this one-inch leaf
floats, suspended over the sidewalk,
sliding a little left, a little right,
then up three inches, down two.
It hangs there an impossibly long time.

Aha! Light just so, I now can see
a nearly invisible thread of silk, spun
by a spider hidden in the tree
above. Does she have a master plan?
Is she fishing for the wind
to carry her thread to the next branch,
to form an anchor for a web work?

Those who pass here later
will never know the web
revealed itself as lace
from the simple use of this leaf
that is only doing what leaves do best—
resting on air, moving in the wind.

Fish Out of Water

I.

Kathy caught a fish in the frog pond once,
a sucker, her dad said, not good to eat.
Removing the hook, she held the sucker
a few moments, watched it struggle to breathe.
Its gills pulsed, then pulsed faster,
the suction-cup mouth searching
for life-giving water. She placed it carefully
back in the pond. Spent, it hesitated,
then swam quickly back to deep water.

She knew how that fish felt.
Once she waded out into the pond.
On her knees, she opened her eyes
to see what fish see, the murky green
like sunlight filtered through hazelnut leaves
when she played in the orchard.
Amazed, she forgot where she was
until, lungs burning, she burst
up into the air, gasping,
to hear her mother calling her to dinner.

II.

Perhaps the first fish that evolved
to take oxygen from air instead of water
understood. Perhaps some impulse in its brain flashed
the picture of a fin levering across solid ground.

That first trip must have been slow,
pectoral fins in opposition, spine flexing,
dorsal fin useless for balance. And all the time
the gasping—the slow pursing of the mouth
and movement of the gills, breathing in
atmosphere alien but sufficient to sustain.

What propelled this sea creature onto the shore,
made its struggle worth the effort?
It left a world of floating lazily through
filtered light with flashes of algae and plankton,
easy eating. But easily eaten.

III.

Kathy remembers her sucker again
seventeen years later. On her way to a job interview,
she starts upstream against the lunchtime crowds
on Montgomery Street, among smartly-dressed
bankers and brokers at home on this street
of buildings taller than silos,
taller even than the grain elevator.

The humid air, the heat from the concrete
offer no comfort. Her breath comes in small gulps.
she has taken the bait, answered the ad, put on
her best cotton dress, sheer stockings, heels.

The man she is about to meet—
will he keep her or throw her back?

Can she ever learn to breathe here?

When It Was Over, No One Clapped

The children sat silent, waiting
for a cue to tell them how
to respond. None came.

As the silence grew, the crowd
eyed neighbors furtively,
shuffled in their seats.

The self-righteous wondered:
If this is the Rapture, when
will I be transported?

The world no longer turned.

The atheists wondered why
they didn't fly into space.
Flying was beyond them now.

The nova's heat lit their faces,
blank, but watchful. They waited, all,
for someone to tell them

what to do next,
where to go,
how to queue up.

No one did.

A child began to spin
in place, then another.
The adults just watched.

Li Po's Crossing

The last glass of sweet rice wine
still washing his warm belly,
he stepped through the gate giggling
to see how the moon had laid her light
atop the Yangtze, framed his small boat
bobbing at the dock. He climbed in,
pushed away, floated in purling
current amid the shimmer.

The bailing bucket caught his eye,
he dipped, filled, spilled
the filament around him
in luminous threads
until the boat was full of silver.
He watched the web of water rippling,
saw how the gleam spread
beyond the boat to Colored Rock Crag.
He reached out to gather it in,
wanting it all to enwrap himself,
then tumbled in rapture
into the river of moonlight.

His silk robes spread around him,
buoyant and gracefully folded.
He gazed at the Cloudy River of the Sky,
watched how it spread out to forever.
With a final sigh he sank
below the surface, drowning
in waves of the moon,
and crossed to the other side.

In the End

When life shatters like a crystal glass
and shards fall around like shaved ice,
when the whole comes apart and separates
and you push pieces around with the toe of your shoe,
this is the end.

Fragments skate across the floor, escape
the wounded fingers that would put them back
together, fingers dripping blood
like drops from a baptismal font.

Baptized by the blood of the broken,
crushed by weight no longer here,
no longer near—
contemplate the afterlife,
the life after, the life taken for granted,
taken like fine drink,
life drunk on itself.

This, then, is the end, to contemplate,
to celebrate the shards and own the whole,
to hear the silver tinkle of a laugh
sliding from the sky.

for Grace

It is here for just a moment,
this mica butterfly captured in stone.
Light angle just right, it flies
into my consciousness,
a spirit released,
bathes me in fragile grace.

I shift my head and it is gone.

The stone is now a plain gray rock,
one of thousands on this Wallowa shore.
Its captive spirit has flown,
climbing a God-beam to the sun.

MARIANNE KLEKACZ lives and writes in Oregon's Coast Range Mountains. A native of Oregon, she returned there after a journey that took her from the wilds of Alaska to the deserts of Arizona, to San Francisco, Switzerland, Denmark, England, The Philippines, the Caribbean Islands, and through many of the fifty states. She has been a cowgirl, policewoman, racecar driver, lifeguard, and a technical specialist in computers and telecommunications. She never met an astronomical phenomenon she didn't want to know more about or a logic puzzle she didn't feel compelled to try to solve. She helps nurture (with husband Ben) 100 acres of mixed-tree forest. A river runs through it. Any or all of these things are likely to show up in her poems.

Marianne's first chapbook, *Life Science*, won the Edna Meudt Memorial Award in 2003. She was awarded a B.A. in English and Writing from Marylhurst University, and an M.F.A. in Writing from Pacific University.

A few words in praise of poets

This book (and many of the poems in it) would never have seen the light of day without the help of a lot of people. Knowing I am undoubtedly omitting someone very important, I'd still like to say a special "thank you" to a few folks:

Cindy Hanson, Ruth Harrison, and Carla Perry, sisters in The Covenant of the Singular Eye, whose challenges provoked some of these poems.

Tuesdays, the central Oregon Coast writing group, for their thoughtful critiques and encouragement.

The many poets who have mentored and encouraged me over the years, including Eleanor Berry, Sharon Bryan, Ger Killeen, Dorianne Laux, Joe Millar, Paulann Petersen, Pattiann Rogers, Vern Rutsala, Peter Sears, and Sandra Williams.

I owe you all immense gratitude.